Islam is one of the world's largest religions. It has followers in countries all around the world. How did it start? What's it a[bout?] Read on and learn more!

THE BEGINNINGS OF ISLAM

Muhammad was an Arab with no particular religious training. He was a merchant. Muslims believe that God selected Muhammad as God's final prophet, and taught Muhammad the true worship of God.

WHAT IS ISLAM?

INTERESTING FACTS ABOUT THE RELIGION OF MUSLIMS

History Book for 6th Grade
Children's Islam Books

BABY PROFESSOR
EDUCATION KIDS

Prophet Muhammad

Muhammad founded the new religion, Islam, in 610 in Arabia. The new religion unified the Arab world, both in worship and politically. By 750, followers of Islam had conquered lands far beyond Arabia, reaching as far as Spain in the west and into what is now Iraq and Iran in the east.

Islam spread partly by conquest. Those in the conquered lands were invited to become Muslims; however, they could usually continue to follow their own faith if they chose. They would have to pay a non-believers' tax, but otherwise were in general left in peace.

Mosque in Nigeria

To learn what everyday life was like for the early Muslims, read the Baby Professor book, The Daily Life of Muslims During the Largest Empire in History.

WHAT DOES "ISLAM" MEAN?

"Islam" is based on the word "Salam", which means "peace". Islam means "the free surrender of your will to the true will of God so you can gain peace."

A Muslim, literally, is anything that practices islam, surrendering to the true will of God. In that sense, every plant, animal, and star in the sky practices islam. They are doing the things for which God created them.

Christians, Jews, and Muslims all agree that people are in a different position from trees or rocks. God loves them, and they have "free will": they can choose how to live their lives. The question is, will they seek to live their lives as God wills, or will they follow their own desires, fears, or things that tempt them, so they end up doing what is far from God's will?

WHAT ISLAM TEACHES

Islam is the worship of one God, the same God that Christians and Jews worship. Those who worship the one God also try to live as God would have them live. Muslims call God, ``Allah''.

Muslims believe that Allah is loving and merciful, that Allah knows all things, even the secret reasons we hold in our heads and hearts for doing what we do. Allah can punish those who do wrong, but desires instead to offer mercy.

The Islamic faith can be summed up in six points. Each Muslim is called to believe in:

- ➤ The one God, Allah.
- ➤ The teachings of the true prophets, including Muhammad.
- ➤ The original writings revealed to Moses, David, Jesus, and Muhammad.
- ➤ The angels.
- ➤ That there is a coming day of Judgment, when evil people will be punished and good people will go on to a new life.
- ➤ That Allah has a plan for each person's life, and that that plan forms the person's destiny.

DOES ISLAM TEACH VIOLENCE?

Islam forbids violence when it is not necessary. No Muslim is to hurt or even threaten another person, unless it is fighting against soldiers of another army.

Some who follow Islam commit acts of violence or terrorism, but Christians and Jews have done similar horrible acts. Violent people sometimes claim they are acting the way God wants them to, but no major religion supports, permits, or praises acts of terrorism, unnecessary violence, or even disrespect of other people.

People who engage in violence to support what they understand about God are sometimes called ``fanatics''. Fanatics are not doing what God wills, but rather are following some twisted interpretation of the will of God. A Muslim fanatic, just like a Christian or a Jewish fanatic, is deeply mistaken in his faith and is dishonoring God through his actions.

Sheikh Zayed Grand Mosque in Abu Dhabi

Quran

THE SACRED BOOKS

Muslims accept that both Christians and Jews received revelations from God, and that those revelations were written in the sacred texts of Jews and Christians. We know those texts as the Old and New Testament.

However, Muslims believe that those texts became corrupt over many years, and that to follow what the current versions of the texts teach is not the best way to live as Allah wants. Muslims believe that Allah provided the Qu'ran through Muhammad to restore the most clear and correct teaching of Allah's will. Muslims further believe that the text of the Qu'ran is without error, and has not changed since Muhammad shared it with the world.

Children reading Quran

Muslims believe that we can learn about Allah through the Qu'ran. For example, there we can find 99 names of God. The names are like descriptions of what God does: among the names, Allah is All-Merciful, the Protector, and the Source of All Peace.

Imagine that, somehow, every printed Qu'ran in the world was destroyed. The Qur'an would still exist! That is because ˝hafiz˝, or ˝guardians˝, have memorized the Qu'ran from beginning to end. There are millions of hafiz around the world, living protectors and sharers of the Qu'ran.

Muslim praying

HOW MUSLIMS WORSHIP

For Muslims, worship is not just going to a religious building and praying. Worship includes both prayers and actions: the prayers help you get stronger in the way of following God's will, and once you know more about what God wants, you can act. Without the prayers, the actions are random. Without the actions, the prayers are just words.

MUSLIMS WORSHIP GOD IN FIVE WAYS:

1. They declare that they believe in One God, and that Muhammad is a prophet of God.
2. The take part in formal prayers five times a day. If they can, they gather with other Muslims at a mosque or in a public place like a park or on a riverbank. If they are alone at the times of prayer, they still pray.
3. The give money to help the needy. Muslims are called to give 2.5% of all the money they earn be-yond what they need for the necessities of food,

Muslim wearing ihram clothes

During the month of Ramadan (it happens at a slightly different time each year because the Muslim calendar is a little different from the calendar the rest of the world uses), Muslims neither eat nor drink between sunrise and sunset.

If they are physically able and can afford it, all Muslims travel to Mecca, in Saudi Arabia, at least once in their lives. Mecca is considered the physical center of Islam, and the visit is called ˝the hajj˝. The rituals of the hajj are based on the struggles of Abraham and his family as they learned to follow God.

Kaaba Mecca Saudi Arabia

Muslims don't worship or pray to the Prophet Muhammad. Muslims respect and honor Muhammad, but they only worship and pray to Allah.

During their five daily prayers, Muslims face Mecca. In Mecca is "the Kaaba", a stone that is the focus for all Muslims. They do not pray to the stone, but concentrate on the Kaaba together so all Muslims can focus their prayers together to honor Allah.

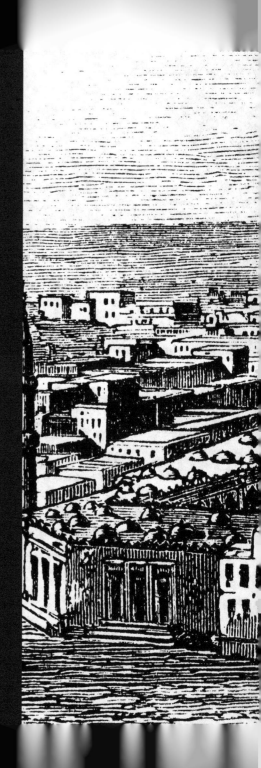

Kaaba Mecca Saudi Arabia

ISLAM IN THEORY AND PRACTICE

There are some ways that Islamic nations and people do not always follow what Islam teaches. This is also true for some Christian nations and people not following what Jesus teaches.

For example, although the Qu'ran speaks of the rights of women and teaches honoring all women, in practice women in many Islamic nations have very restricted rights. This is not really because of the teachings of Islam, but because of cultural traditions in male-dominated societies.

Sometimes women are attacked for trying to go to school, or for not wearing the right clothing, including a scarf to cover their heads. Women respond that wearing the head scarf should be their free choice to accept a way of dressing modestly in public, not something men force them to do.

In theory, an Islamic nation would tolerate those who worship God in a different way, as long as they pay the required tax. In practice, in many Islamic countries, followers of other religions, and even followers of certain branches of Islam, are in danger of being arrested, jailed, attacked, or even killed. The Qu'ran does not teach this, but many Muslims feel that non-believers are insulting Islam by acting as they do, and the more hot-headed of these people sometimes take violent actions.

Basharat Mosque

Some Muslim leaders sometimes declare "jihad", which they or others say is a "holy war" either against non-believers or against Muslims who are behaving in some way the leaders do not like. In the Qu'ran, "jihad" means "to struggle to surrender to God's will". Fighting and killing people sometimes has to happen in wars, but God's will is more about correcting the pride, laziness, and anger in one's own heart, and in reaching out to those in need.

FINDING GOD'S PEOPLE

People all over the world seek to do God's will, and try to become closer to God by following the teachings of their religion.

Interested to know more about a Christian seeker of God's will? Read another Baby Professor book, `A Rich Man in Poor Clothes: The Story of St. Francis of Assisi`.

Visit

BABY PROFESSOR
EDUCATION KIDS

www.BabyProfessorBooks.com

to download Free Baby Professor eBooks
and view our catalog of new and exciting
Children's Books

9 781541 913660